BOONE COUNTY LIBRARY
D0288115

Perfect Phrases in American Sign Language for Beginners

WITHDRAWN

BOONE COUNTY PUBLIC LIBRARY
BURLINGTON, KY 41005
www.bcpl.org

SEP 28 2009

Perfect Phrases in American Sign Language for Beginners

150 ESSENTIAL PHRASES
FOR COMMUNICATING WITH USERS OF ASL

•

Lou Fant
and
Barbara Bernstein Fant

•

Illustrations by Betty G. Miller

•

McGraw Hill

New York Chicago San Francisco Lisbon London Madrid Mexico City
Milan New Delhi San Juan Seoul Singapore Sydney Toronto

The McGraw-Hill Companies

Library of Congress Cataloging-in-Publication Data

Fant, Louie J.
Perfect phrases in American Sign Language for beginners / Lou Fant and Barbara Bernstein Fant ; illustrations by Betty G. Miller.
p. cm.
Includes index.
0-07-159877-4 (alk. paper)
1. American Sign Language.

HV2475 .F37 2008
419'.7—dc22 2008012718

Copyright © 2009 by Estate of Lou Fant and Barbara Bernstein Fant. All rights reserved. Printed in the United States of America. Except as permitted under the United States Copyright Act of 1976, no part of this publication may be reproduced or distributed in any form or by any means, or stored in a database or retrieval system, without the prior written permission of the publisher.

1 2 3 4 5 6 7 8 9 10 11 12 13 14 15 16 17 18 19 20 21 22 FGR/FGR 0 9

ISBN 978-0-07-159877-4
MHID 0-07-159877-4

The publisher would like to thank Darren Fudenske and Melanie Schneider for their help.

McGraw-Hill books are available at special quantity discounts to use as premiums and sales promotions or for use in corporate training programs. To contact a representative, please visit the Contact Us pages at www.mhprofessional.com.

This book is printed on acid-free paper.

Contents

Preface vii
Acknowledgments ix

Chapter 1 Basic Sentence Types 1
Chapter 2 Question Signs 3
Chapter 3 Greetings, Introductions, and Common Expressions 9
Chapter 4 Getting Better Acquainted 27
Chapter 5 Signing and Deafness 45
Chapter 6 Health 61
Chapter 7 Numbers, Time, Dates, and Money 81
Chapter 8 Technology 103
Chapter 9 Holidays and Occasions 117
Chapter 10 Additional Vocabulary 123

Appendix: The Manual Alphabet 156

Preface

This book is designed to provide various phrases for beginning learners of American Sign Language or those who wish to communicate with the Deaf. American Sign Language is the dominant sign language of the Deaf community in the United States and English-speaking parts of Canada. Here are some key phrases for everyday communication concerning greetings, introductions, signing and deafness, health, numbers, time, money, and more—in short, basic survival phrases in American Sign Language.

This book is not meant to teach the fundamentals of ASL grammar or offer a comprehensive array of phrases (longer discussions of ASL grammar and basics can be found elsewhere, and almost 500 phrases can be found in *The American Sign Language Phrase Book, Third Edition*). Even so, those who consistently use these basic phrases may discover that they begin to understand some sign concepts and can build upon this foundation to continue learning American Sign Language.

It is important to be aware that American Sign is a visual-spatial language distinct from spoken English. It has its own grammar, and the order in which signs are put together is different from English. ASL grammar incorporates not only the use of facial expressions but head and body movements and the efficient use of space around the signer as well.

Acknowledgments

I wish to convey my heartfelt appreciation to Dave A. Morrison, my dear friend and colleague at Seattle Central Community College, for his spirited perusal of this book and suggested changes

I extend my gratitude once more to Holly McGuire at McGraw-Hill for her guidance and assistance on this project.

And to my mother, Rita Bernstein, thank you for the life lessons you have taught me. All my love to you.

Perfect Phrases in American Sign Language for Beginners

Chapter 1

Basic Sentence Types

As I mentioned earlier in the Introduction chapter, facial expressions play a very significant role in ASL. In a spoken language, the rise and fall of the voice adds meaning to the words spoken. Imagine the various ways one can say "I love you." The characteristic rising of the voice toward the end of a question is another example. Facial expressions are to ASL as vocal inflection is to spoken English.

Throughout this book, you will note that the phrases are delineated as statements or questions. The face has these duties and supplies additional subtleties and nuances of meaning. Signs have meanings in and of themselves just as words do, but these meanings are altered, shaped, enriched, and amplified by facial expressions. This Is true especially when one asks questions in ASL. In general, when one asks a *wh-* sign (who, what, why, where, when, which, how, and how many or how much—see Chapter 2), the eyebrows are downward. All other questions usually cause the eyebrows to move upward—for example, questions that require an affirmative or negative response. To support an affirmative response, nodding of the head would occur, e.g., "Yes, I'm married," or a shaking of the head with the "I'm not married" response.

For a *wh-* sign question, the eyebrows usually go downward. The *wh-* sign question is also accompanied by a head tilt.

Eyebrows move upward for other questions and are usually accompanied by a head tilt.

Chapter 2

Question Signs

The *wh-* sign may come at the beginning or at the end of a question, or it may appear in both places. If you wish to emphasize a question, place it at the end.

WHO

WHAT SHRUG

WHAT

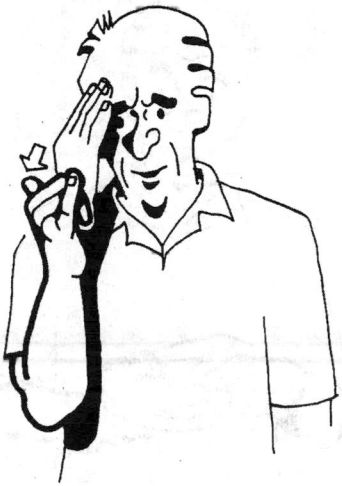

WHY

WHERE

WHEN

WHICH

HOW

HOW MANY/HOW MUCH

Chapter 3

Greetings, Introductions, and Common Expressions

Hello.

HELLO

Good morning.

GOOD

MORNING

Good afternoon.

GOOD

AFTERNOON

Good night.

GOOD

NIGHT

I'm glad to see you.

HAPPY

SEE

Good-bye.

GOOD-BYE

Please.

PLEASE

Yes.

YES

No.

NO

Thank you.

GOOD

Excuse me.

EXCUSE

It's all right. It's okay.

ALL RIGHT

I'm sorry.

SORRY

What is your name?

NAME WHAT SHRUG

My name is _____.

I NAME

Fingerspell your name.

It's nice to meet you.

NICE

MEET

Where do you live?

LIVE

WHERE

Where are you from?

FROM

WHERE

Are you in school?

SCHOOL

YOU

I'm a student.

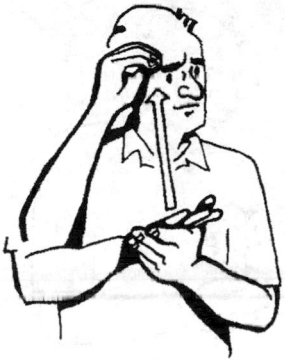

LEARN

AGENT

I

AGENT is a sign used in conjunction with another sign in order to designate a person who does a particular thing. The AGENT sign can be used with most but not all occupations

What kind of work do you do?

WORK

MAJOR

WHAT SHRUG

I'm a doctor.

I

DOCTOR

I'm a lawyer/teacher.

LAW

TEACH

He knows me.

HE/SHE/IT

KNOWS

ME

Verbs in ASL fall into three categories: nondirectional verbs, one-directional verbs, and multidirectional verbs. Movement in verb signs may express who is performing an action (the subject) and to whom the action is directed (the direct object). This quality of movement is called verb directionality

The nondirectional verbs (like the one above) do not express either subject or direct object; therefore, these two things (subject and direct object nouns and pronouns) must be supplied.

I love you.

I

LOVE

YOU

This is also a nondirectional verb.

I see him/her/it.

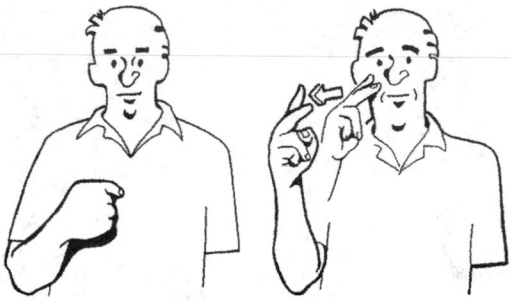

I SEE

In regard to verb directionality, as seen in this example one-directional verb signs express direct object but not subject; that is, one-directional verbs move toward the direct object; thus, a noun or pronoun is not required.

I help you.

HELP

Here we see an example of a multidirectional verb sign in which the movement goes from the subject toward the direct object; thus, neither subject nor direct object is signed.

You tell me.

YOU

TELL ME

This is another one-directional verb sign.

Can you give me the time?

YOU

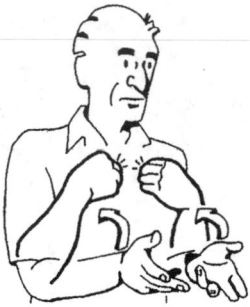

GIVE ME

TIME

CAN

Chapter 4

Getting Better Acquainted

How are you?

HOW

YOU

Fine.

FINE

Additional vocabulary:

I am sick/tired/wonderful.

SICK

TIRED

WONDERFUL

Are you married?

MARRY

YOU

Yes, I'm married.

YES

MARRY

ME

May I introduce my wife?

INTRODUCE WIFE

Additional vocabulary:

May I introduce my husband/son/daughter/friend?

HUSBAND

SON

DAUGHTER

FRIEND

After making the sign for the person you are introducing, you then fingerspell that person's name.

I'm single.

I

ONLY

I'm divorced.

I

DIVORCED

Do you have any children?

CHILDREN

HAVE

YOU

Have you eaten? Did you eat? Are you finished eating?

EAT

FINISH

I haven't eaten yet.

EAT

LATE

I

Are you hungry?

HUNGER

YOU

Let's you and I go to a restaurant.

YOU AND I

GO TO

RESTAURANT

What are you going to order?

ORDER WHAT SHRUG

I will order breakfast.

EAT

MORNING

ORDER

WILL

I

Lunch/dinner

EAT

NOON

EAT

NIGHT

She can't go.

WOMAN

GO TO

CAN'T

HE/SHE/IT

Do you have a car?

CAR

HAVE

May I go with you?

I

WITH

Come visit me sometime.

ONLY

TIME

COME

VISIT

Chapter 5

Signing and Deafness

I'm learning sign language.

I **LEARN** **SIGN** **LANGUAGE**

Sign slowly, please.

SIGN

SLOW

PLEASE

Please repeat.

AGAIN

PLEASE

I can fingerspell, but I can't read it well.

FINGERSPELL

CAN

BUT

READ

GOOD

CAN'T

You sign fast.

SIGN

RAPID

YOU

I understand.

I UNDERSTAND

I don't understand.

UNDERSTAND

Would you write it, please?

WRITE

PLEASE

How do you sign _____? What's the sign for _____?

SIGN

HOW

Ask these questions by pointing to whatever it is you want to know the sign for or by fingerspelling the word.

There's no sign for that; you have to fingerspell it.

SIGN

HAVE

NONE

FINGERSPELL

MUST

What does _____ mean?

MEAN

WHAT SHRUG

To ask this question, first make the sign of whatever it is that you want to know the meaning of, then sign MEAN WHAT SHRUG.

Are you deaf?

DEAF (A)

DEAF (B)

YOU

Either way of signing "deaf" is acceptable.

I'm not deaf; I'm hearing.

DEAF

NOT

SPEAK

I

I'm hard of hearing.

HARD OF HEARING

I

Do you use a hearing aid?

HEARING AID

USE

YOU

Can you read lips?

LIPREAD

CAN

YOU

I speak a little.

SPEAK

LITTLE BIT

I was born deaf.

BIRTH

DEAF

Chapter 6

Health

How do you feel?

HOW

FEEL

Do you feel all right?

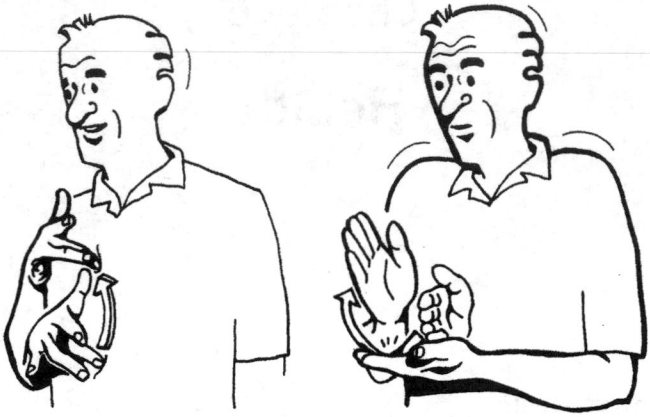

FEEL ALL RIGHT

I don't feel well.

FEEL

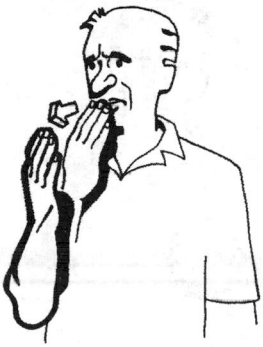

GOOD

NOT

I am sick.

I

SICK

I am really sick.

I

TRUE

SICK

When the signer wishes to stress or emphasize statements, then the TRUE sign is used.

I feel better now.

FEEL

BETTER

NOW

Where is the rest room?

TOILET

WHERE

Wash your hands.

WASH HANDS (1)

WASH HANDS (2)

WASH HANDS (3)

This sign, shown in three steps, is a mime of actually washing the hands.

Wash your face.

WASH FACE

Similarly, this sign is a mime of actually washing the face.

Where does it hurt?

PAIN

WHERE

My head aches.

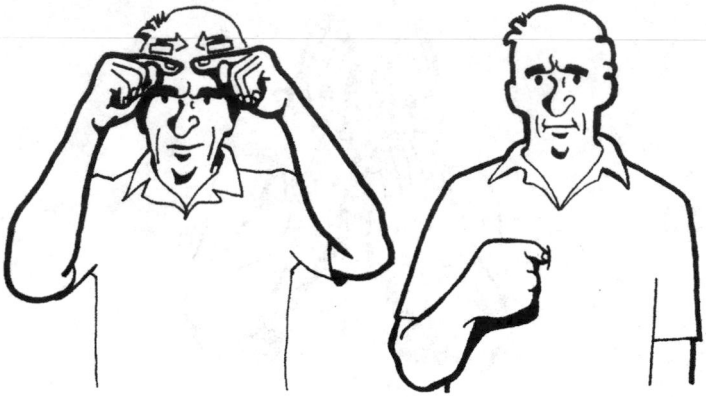

HEADACHE I

I have a toothache.

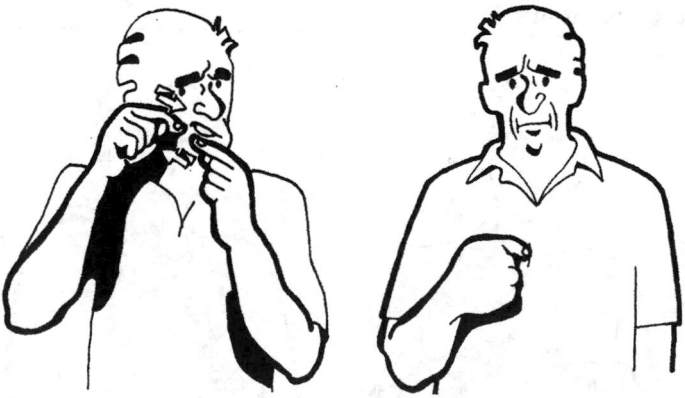

TOOTHACHE I

I have a stomachache.

STOMACHACHE I

The sign PAIN may be placed anywhere on the body to denote that you are hurt or have a pain in that part of your body.

I have a cold.

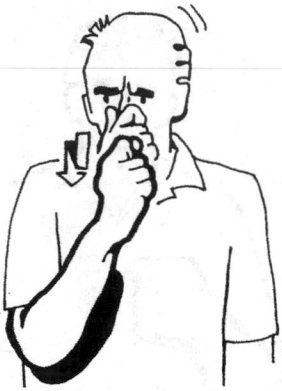

BLOW NOSE

I

Do you have any aspirin?

HAVE

A-S-P-I-R-I-N

Fingerspell ASPIRIN.

I need a dentist/doctor.

DENTIST

DOCTOR

MUST

I

I have to take pills.

PILL

MUST

I've run out of medicine.

MEDICINE

USED UP

It's time to take your temperature.

TIME

FOR

ORAL THERMOMETER

You have to have a shot.

HYPODERMIC

MUST/NEED

YOU

The MUST sign may mean "need" or "should" and is done differently depending on the meaning desired. If something is mandatory, then make one movement down. If something is optional but desirable, then make two gentle downward movements.

You need to have an X-ray.

Fingerspell X-RAY.

Were any bones broken?

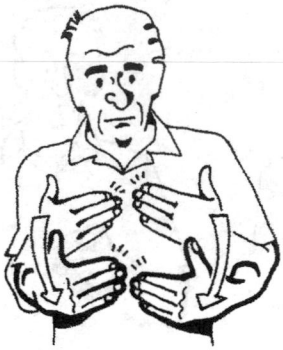

BODY

BREAK

ANY

There is no standard sign for "bone," so the statement here is more generally read as, "Is anything in your body broken?" If you wish to sign "bone" specifically, you must fingerspell it or find out what the local sign for it is.

Call the ambulance.

EMERGENCY VEHICLE

BECKON

The sign for "ambulance" indicates the spinning red light on top of the vehicle and may refer to any emergency vehicle or just the flashing red light itself.

My wife is in the hospital.

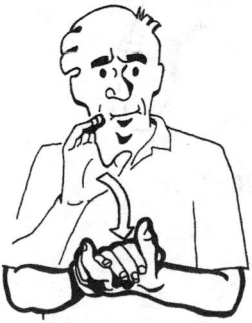

WIFE

HOSPITAL

Any family member or friends sign can be substituted in lieu of WIFE to create new phrases. The HOSPITAL sign is made by drawing a cross on the sleeve.

Do you have hospitalization insurance?

HOSPITAL

INSURANCE

HAVE

Chapter 7

Numbers, Time, Dates, and Money

See Chapter 10 for additional vocabulary in numbers, time, and money.

What's your phone number?

PHONE **NUMBER** **WHAT SHRUG**

My phone number is _____.

MY

PHONE

NUMBER

Fingerspell your phone number after the sign NUMBER. (See Chapter 10 for number signs.)

What time is it?

TIME

It is 4:45.

TIME

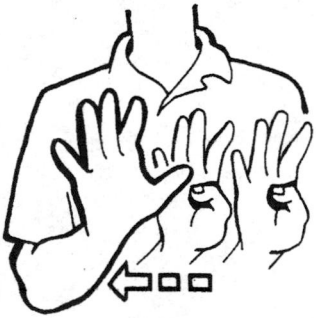

4-4-5

It is 6:15.

TIME

6-15

I have an appointment at 2:30.

APPOINTMENT

TIME

2-30

How old are you?

OLD

YOU

He is 87 years old.

HE/SHE/IT

OLD

87

My birthday is April 3, 1948.

MY

BIRTH

DAY

A-P-R-I-L

3

19-48

The months of March, April, May, June, and July are spelled out. Months with more letters are abbreviated in fingerspelling.

I'll see you next Monday.

SEE

NEAR FUTURE

MONDAY

He goes to the movies every Tuesday.

EVERY TUESDAY

GO TO

MOVIE

HE/SHE/IT

By moving the sign for a day of the week downward, as done with TUESDAY here, you convey the idea of every week on that day.

I see her every Saturday.

EVERY SATURDAY SEE

I visited my aunt two months ago.

TWO MONTHS

PAST

AUNT

VISIT

I bought a new house two years ago.

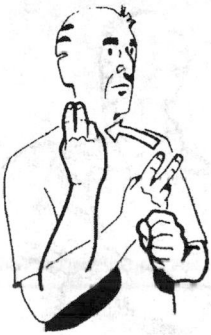

TWO YEARS AGO

BUY

NEW

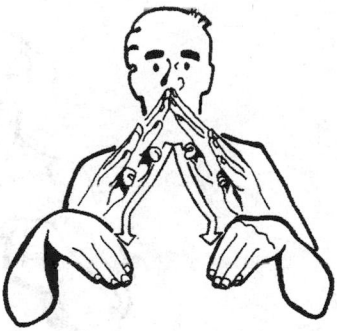

HOUSE

I graduate in two years.

TWO YEARS FROM NOW

GRADUATE

I

I pay every three months.

PAY

EVERY THREE MONTHS

How much does the book cost?

BOOK

COST

HOW MANY

How much did you pay?

PAY

HOW MANY

Have you a nickel/dime/quarter?

5¢

10¢

25¢

HAVE

I have no money.

MONEY

HAVE

NONE

I'm broke.

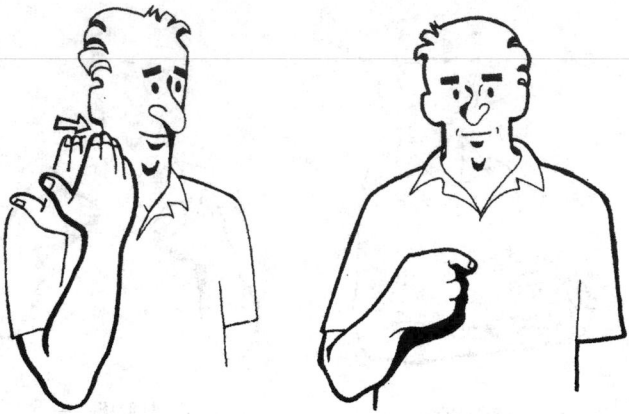

BROKE

I

How much does she owe?

OWE

HOW MANY

HE/SHE/IT

Chapter 8

Technology

Would you mind giving me your e-mail address?

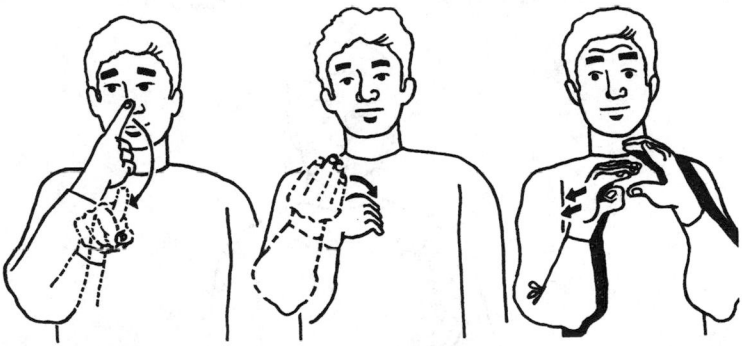

DON'T MIND **GIVE ME** **E-MAIL**

I need to recharge my mobile phone.

MOBILE PHONE

PLUG IN

MUST/NEED

Mine's a BlackBerry/phone.

MOBILE PHONE

MY

B-B (BLACKBERRY)

Fingerspell "B-B."

Deaf people text message their hearing friends.

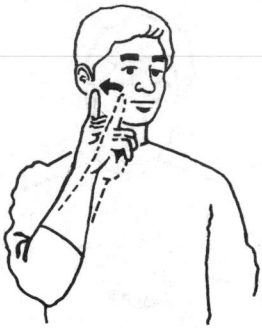

DEAF

PEOPLE

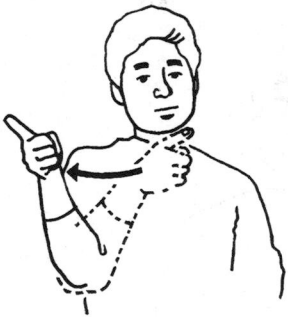

THEY

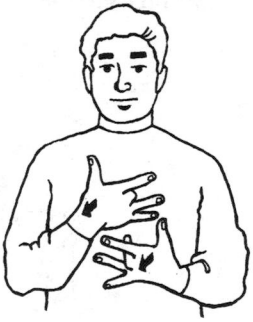

TEND TO

HEARING

FRIEND

T-E-X-T

SEND

Fingerspell "TEXT."

Most deaf people are using video relay services rather than TTYs.

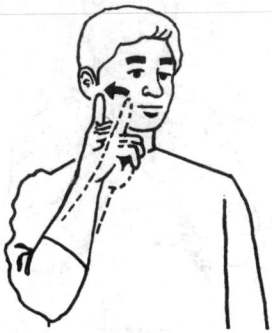

DEAF

ALL OVER

T-T-Y

LESS

Fingerspell "T-T-Y."

NOW

VIDEO RELAY

When you get home, check your video relay mail.

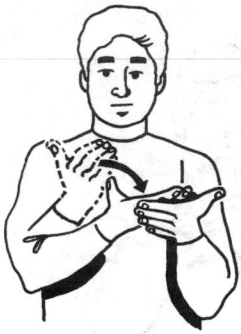

ARRIVE

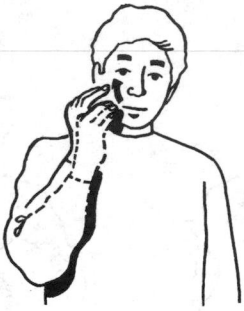

HOME

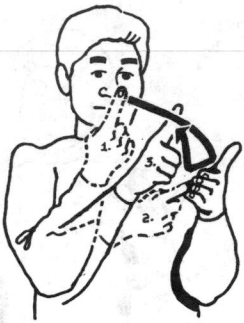

CHECK

COMPUTER

VIDEO RELAY

MESSAGE

There are many different signs for computer (see also page 114).

My TV has closed captioning.

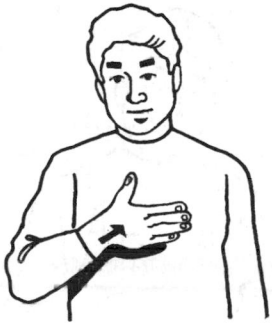

MY

T-V

(CLOSE) SENTENCE

HE/SHE/IT

Fingerspell "T-V."

He/she has a high-definition TV.

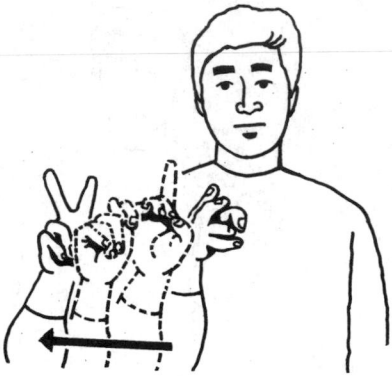

H-D-T-V

HAVE

HE/SHE/IT

Fingerspell "H-D-T-V."

Where's the remote?

REMOTE CONTROL

WHERE

What make is your computer?

COMPUTER YOUR

NAME

Note this sign for computer.

Download this program.

PROGRAM DOWNLOAD

Please save your file.

FILE

SAVE

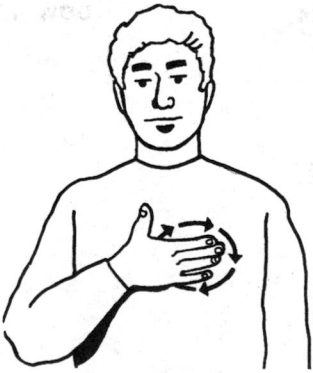

PLEASE

Chapter 9

Holidays and Occasions

Happy birthday.

HAPPY BIRTH DAY

Have a nice Thanksgiving.

HAVE

NICE

THANKSGIVING (1)

THANKSGIVING (2)

Merry Christmas.

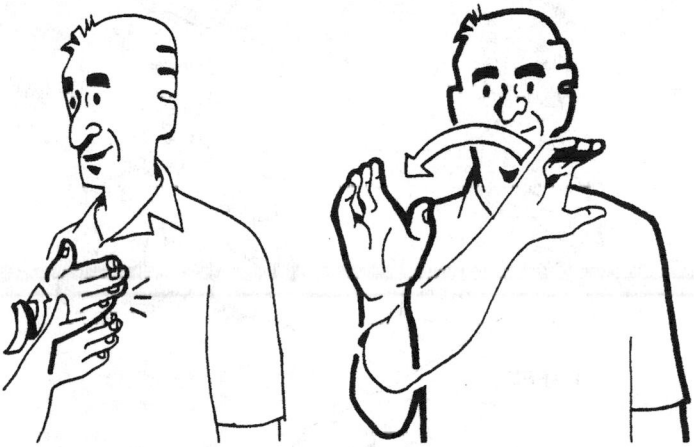

HAPPY **CHRISTMAS**

Note: for Christmas Eve, the word *Eve* is fingerspelled.

Happy New Year.

HAPPY

NEW

YEAR

Note: For New Year's Eve, the word *Eve* is fingerspelled.

Happy Passover.

HAPPY

CRACKER (PASSOVER)

Happy Hanukkah.

HAPPY

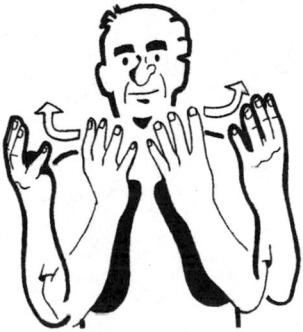

HANNUKAH

Happy Fourth of July.

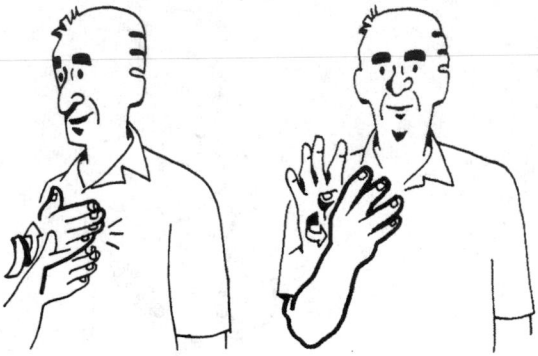

HAPPY 4TH J-U-L-Y

Fingerspell JULY.

Chapter 10

Additional Vocabulary

Miscellaneous Key Vocabulary

FINISH

FINISH

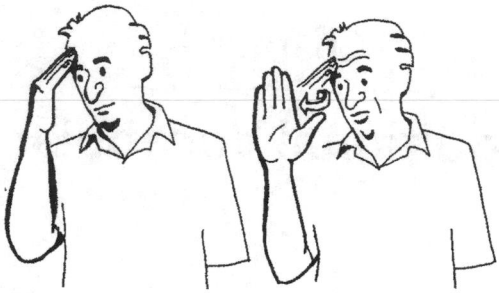

KNOW **DON'T KNOW**

LIKE **DON'T LIKE**

These three verb signs (KNOW, LIKE, and WANT) have negation built into them. The signer should always shake the head while simultaneously making the negative form of the sign.

WANT DON'T WANT

Pronouns

I/ME

YOU

HE/SHE/IT

THEY

MY

HIS/HER/ITS

YOUR

OUR

THEIR

Family Signs

Our family is large/small.

OUR

FAMILY

LARGE

SMALL

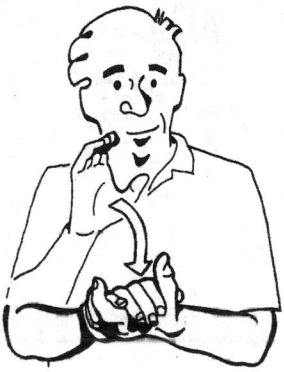

WIFE

HUSBAND

SON

DAUGHTER

FRIEND

FATHER

MOTHER

BROTHER

SISTER

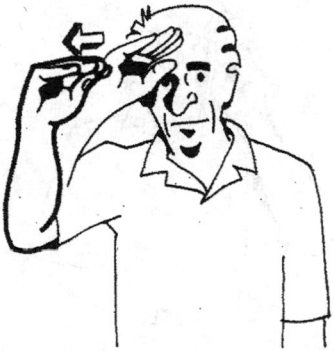

MAN

WOMAN

GIRL

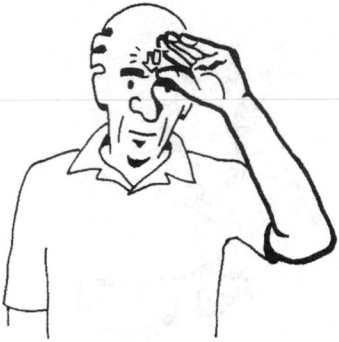

BOY

AUNT

UNCLE

Numbers

0 (ZERO)

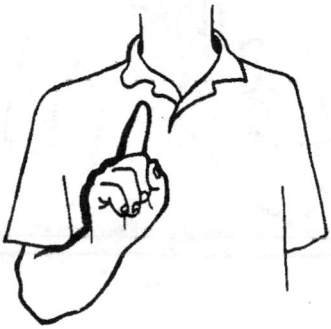

1

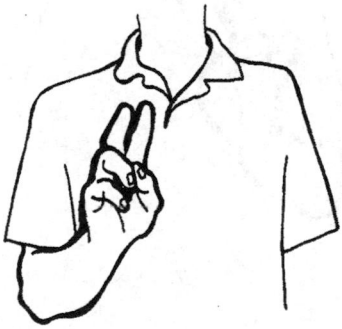

2

3

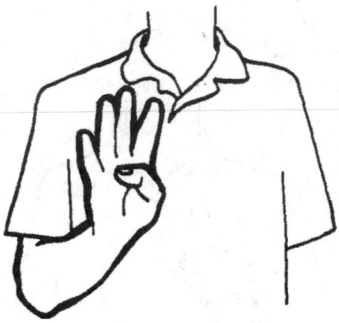

4

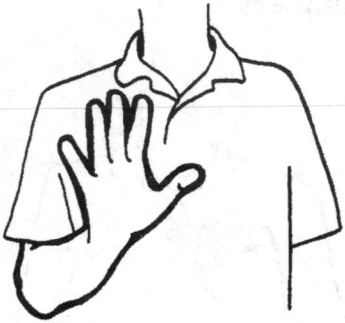

5

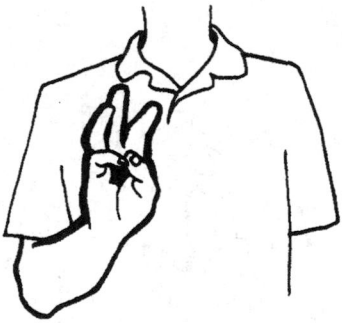

6

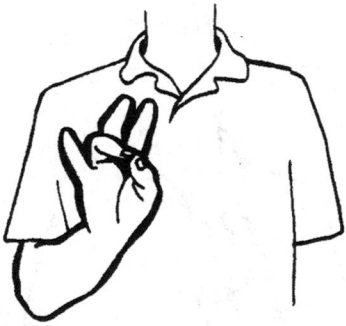

7

The signs for the number 6 and the letter *W* are exactly the same. Context tells you whether the number or the letter is intended.

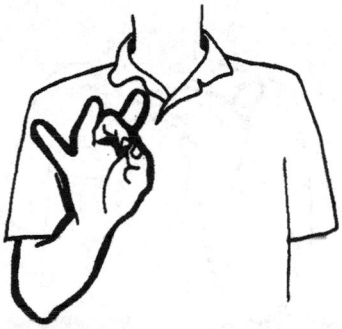

8

9

10

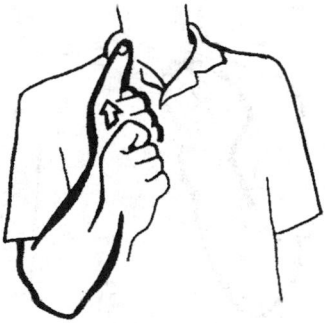

11

The sign for the number 9 is the same as that for the letter *F*.

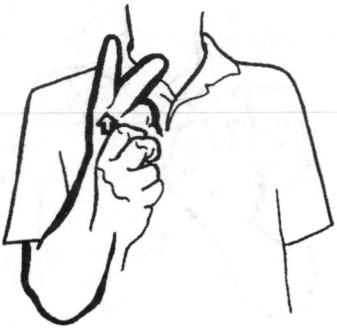

12

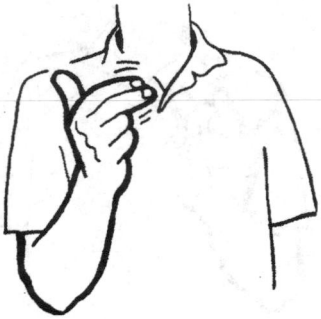

13

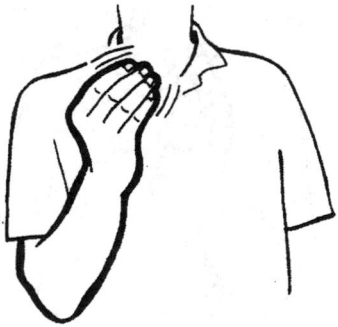

14

15

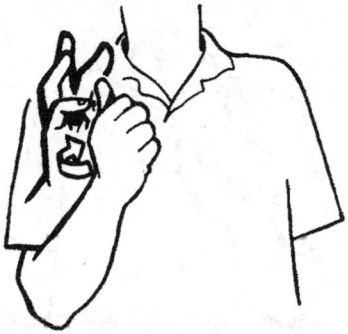

16

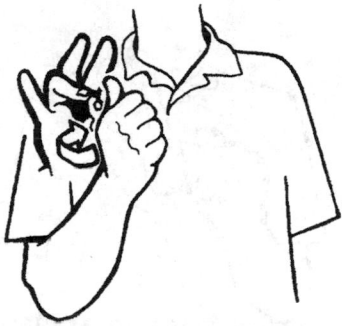

17

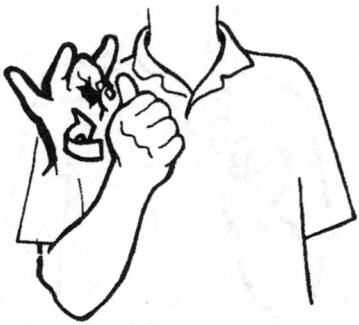

18

19

The numbers 16 through 19 are actually a very fast blend of 10 and 6, 10 and 7, 10 and 8, and 10 and 9.

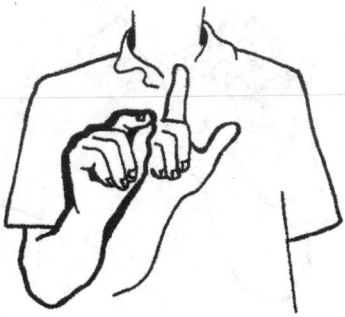

20

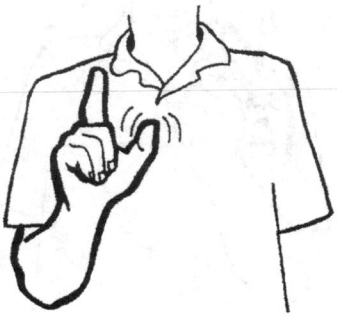

21

22

23

That the 2 in the twenties is made with the thumb and index finger rather than the index and middle finger—as it appears in the number 22—is probably due to the fact that ASL has its roots in the old French sign language. In Europe, even hearing people count *one* with the thumb and *two* with the thumb and index finger.

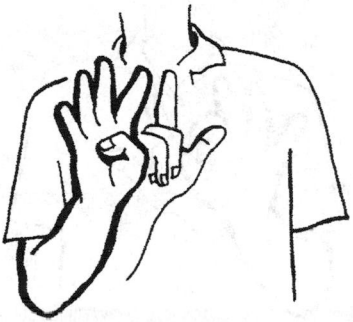

24

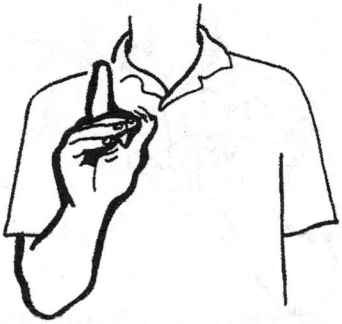

25

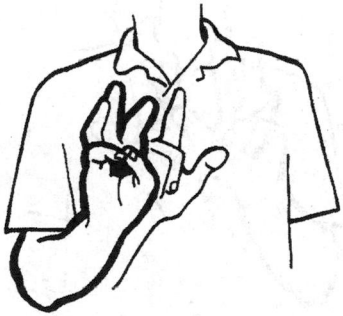

26

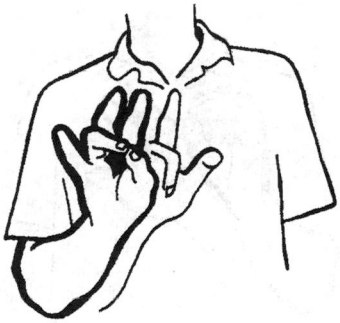

27

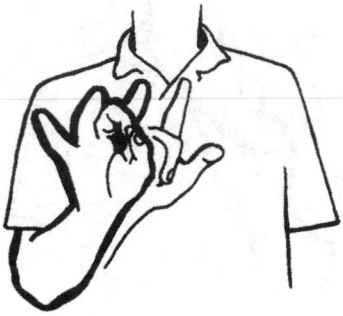

28

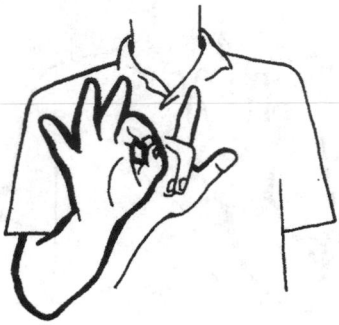

29

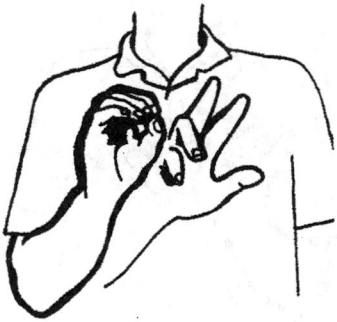

30

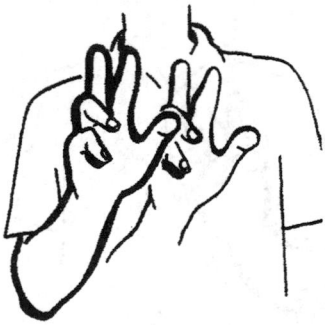

33

The numbers from 30 through 99 are done with the numbers 0 through 9.

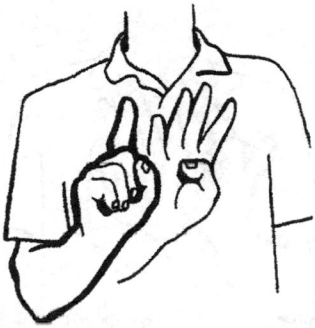

41

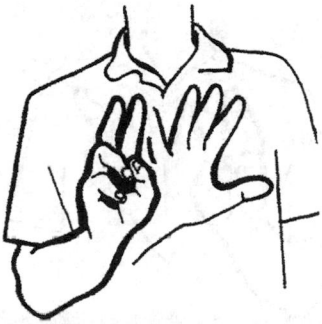

52

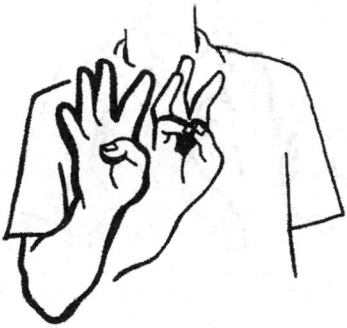

64

75

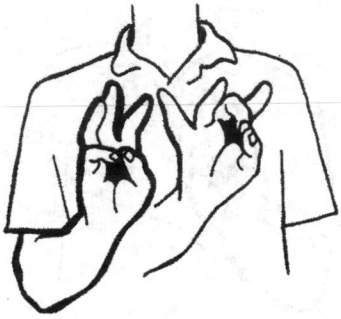

86

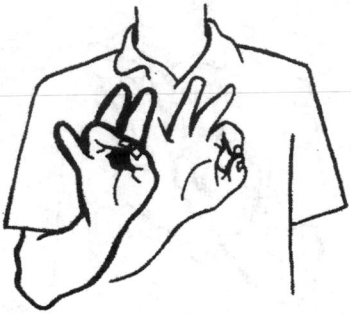

97

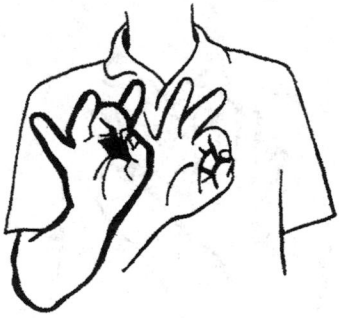

98

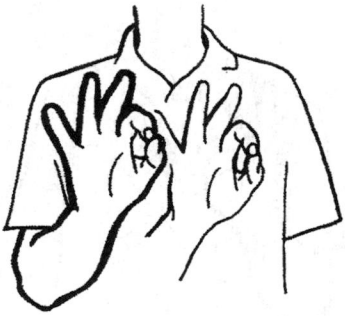

99

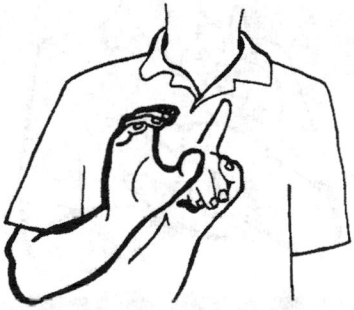

100

The number 100 is made by signing the number 1 and the letter *C*.

777 (A)

777 (B)

The numbers between 100 and 999 are made in one of two ways. One may make the number "7-7-7" or one may sign "7-C-7-7":

1,000

1,000,000

Days of the Week and Seasons

MONDAY

TUESDAY

WEDNESDAY

THURSDAY

FRIDAY

SATURDAY

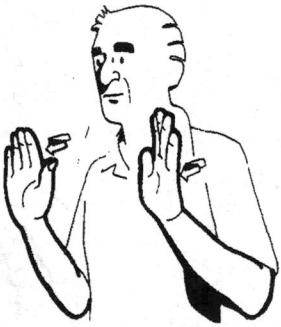

WONDERFUL (SUNDAY)

GROW (SPRING)

SUMMER

AUTUMN

COLD (WINTER)

Money and Ordinals

These signs also serve as ordinal numbers—i.e., first, second, third, etc.

$1.00

$2.00

$3.00

$4.00

$5.00

$6.00

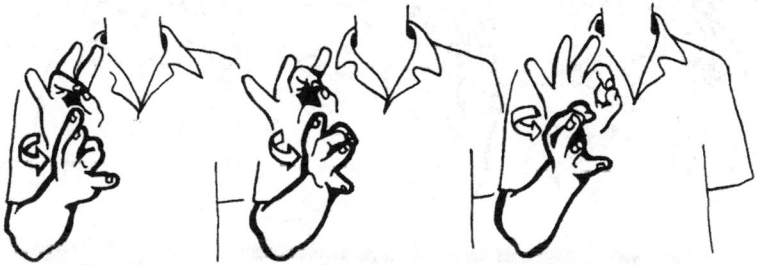

$7.00 **$8.00** **$9.00**

The sign DOLLAR is used when the amount is over nine dollars or when speaking specifically of a bill, as in "a dollar bill." As here:

10 **DOLLAR**

$10.00

1¢

2¢

3¢

4¢

5¢

6¢

7¢

8¢

9¢

10¢

These signs are used only when speaking of these amounts by themselves, not when they are preceded by a dollar amount. For example, $3.09 would be signed as follows:

$3.-0-9

25¢

50¢

The same applies to the two individual cent signs above. Use them only when speaking of these amounts alone, and not with a dollar amount.

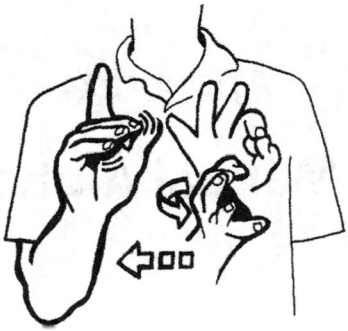

$9.-25

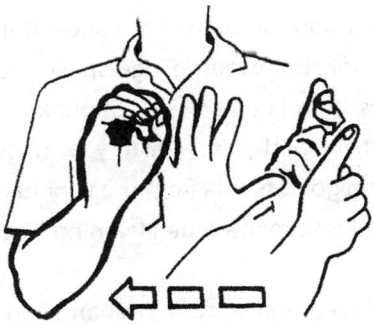

$1.-5-0

Appendix

The Manual Alphabet

When there is not a sign for an idea or concept, then fingerspelling using the manual alphabet occurs. Fingerspelling is used particularly with proper names; brand names; titles of books and movies; names of places and certain foods, etc. Mastery of fingerspelling can be achieved if you form good habits from the very beginning.

Here are some tips to follow when learning fingerspelling:

1. Relax your fingers and, in turn, your arm and shoulder. Tension will impede clear formation of the letters, or "handshapes," as they are called in the manual alphabet.
2. Let your arm hang down with your elbow to your side and your hand slightly in front of you. Do not allow your elbow to move away from your side and rise upward.
3. Do not try to fingerspell rapidly. It is important to maintain a constant rhythm, but do not bounce your hand. Speed will come naturally with time.
4. Pause for one-fourth of a beat at the end of a word if you are fingerspelling several words at a time.

5. Do not *say* the letters or words out loud or to yourself as you make them. Do not develop this habit, otherwise it will be exceedingly difficult to break once established. As you fingerspell a word, *mouth* the whole word. This is done especially with some Deaf people who have been taught to lipread words, not letters.
6. Practice with someone so you can gain experience reading fingerspelling.
7. In reading fingerspelling; look at the whole shape or configuration of the word rather than reading each individual letter or handshape.

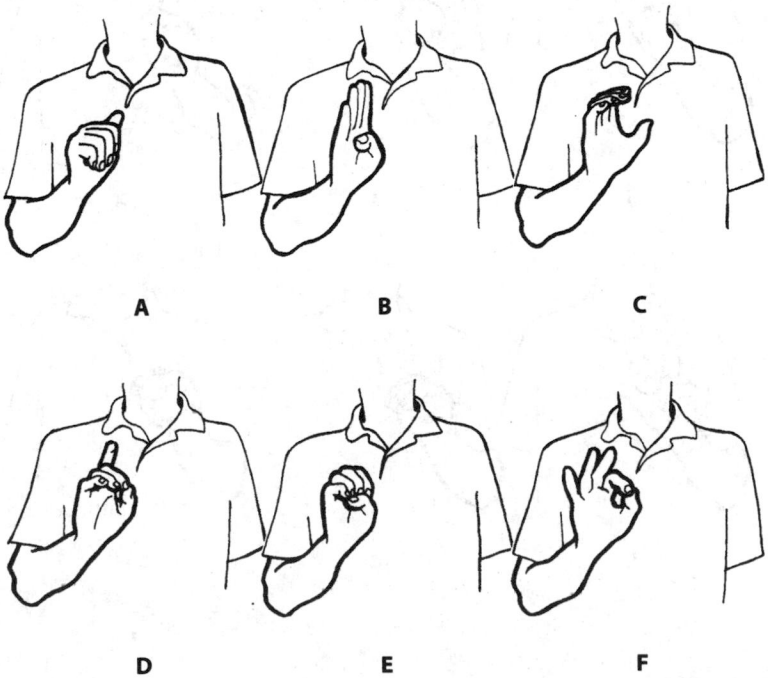

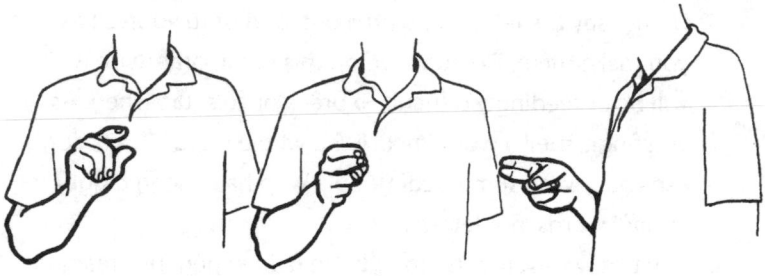

G H H (SIDE VIEW)

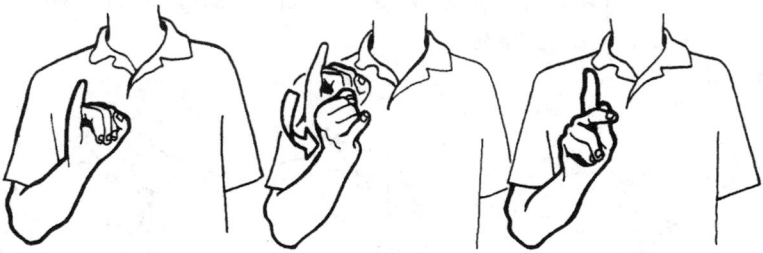

I J K

L M N

O

P

Q

Q (SIDE VIEW)

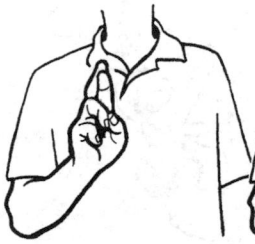

R

S

T

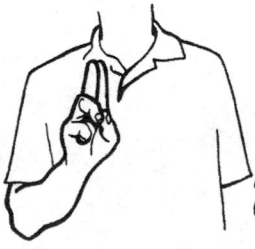

U

V

The sign for the letter *O* is the same as that for the number 0 (zero).

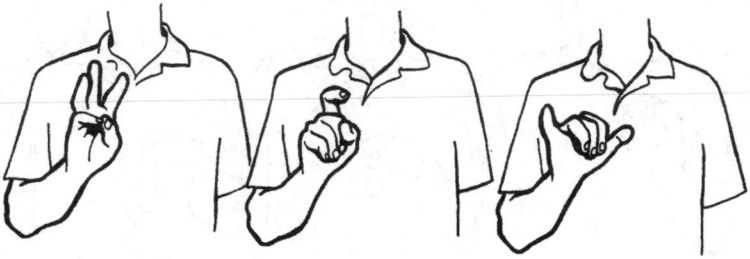

W X Y

Z

The Right Phrase for Every Situation...Every Time.

Perfect Phrases for Building Strong Teams
Perfect Phrases for Business Letters
Perfect Phrases for Business Proposals and Business Plans
Perfect Phrases for Business School Acceptance
Perfect Phrases for College Application Essays
Perfect Phrases for Cover Letters
Perfect Phrases for Customer Service
Perfect Phrases for Dealing with Difficult People
Perfect Phrases for Dealing with Difficult Situations at Work
Perfect Phrases for Documenting Employee Performance Problems
Perfect Phrases for Executive Presentations
Perfect Phrases for Landlords and Property Managers
Perfect Phrases for Law School Acceptance
Perfect Phrases for Lead Generation
Perfect Phrases for Managers and Supervisors
Perfect Phrases for Managing Your Small Business
Perfect Phrases for Medical School Acceptance
Perfect Phrases for Meetings
Perfect Phrases for Motivating and Rewarding Employees
Perfect Phrases for Negotiating Salary & Job Offers
Perfect Phrases for Perfect Hiring
Perfect Phrases for the Perfect Interview
Perfect Phrases for Performance Reviews
Perfect Phrases for Real Estate Agents & Brokers
Perfect Phrases for Resumes
Perfect Phrases for Sales and Marketing Copy
Perfect Phrases for the Sales Call
Perfect Phrases for Setting Performance Goals
Perfect Phrases for Small Business Owners
Perfect Phrases for the TOEFL Speaking and Writing Sections
Perfect Phrases for Writing Grant Proposals
Perfect Phrases in American Sign Language for Beginners
Perfect Phrases in French for Confident Travel
Perfect Phrases in German for Confident Travel
Perfect Phrases in Italian for Confident Travel
Perfect Phrases in Spanish for Confident Travel to Mexico
Perfect Phrases in Spanish for Construction
Perfect Phrases in Spanish for Gardening and Landscaping
Perfect Phrases in Spanish for Household Maintenance and Childcare
Perfect Phrases in Spanish for Restaurant and Hotel Industries

Visit mhprofessional.com/perfectphrases for a complete product listing.

Learn more. Mc Graw Hill Do more.